E. F. Thomas Fortune

A CONCISE AND AUTHENTIC HISTORY OF THE BANK OF ENGLAND

WITH DISSERTATIONS ON METALS AND COIN, BANK NOTES AND BILLS OF

EXCHANGE

E. F. Thomas Fortune

A CONCISE AND AUTHENTIC HISTORY OF THE BANK OF ENGLAND
WITH DISSERTATIONS ON METALS AND COIN, BANK NOTES AND BILLS OF EXCHANGE

ISBN/EAN: 9783742800985

Manufactured in Europe, USA, Canada, Australia, Japa

Cover: Foto ©knipser5 / pixelio.de

Manufactured and distributed by brebook publishing software
(www.brebook.com)

E. F. Thomas Fortune

A CONCISE AND AUTHENTIC HISTORY OF THE BANK OF ENGLAND

PREFACE.

AT a Time like the present, when so many mean Arts are made use of, to mislead the unwary and uninformed, it becomes the Duty of every Individual, however obscure, to contribute his Mite towards promoting the Welfare of his Country; this, and this only, has induced the Author of the following little Treatise, to endeavour to place Things upon their right Foundation; to UNMASK FACTION; and to oppose Truth to Misrepresentation. It will be found in the perusal of the following Pages, that the present Situation of the Bank of England is by no Means new, or without precedent: the Rebellion in the Year 1745, produced the same Effect, but with much more Reason for it then, than now. By comparing the different Degrees of Dangers at that Time and this, and the several Steps taken to support the Bank at both Periods, the Reader, it is supposed and hoped, will be able to draw his own Conclusions, and decide to a certainty whether at this Period there is real Cause for the great Alarm that has been diffused throughout the Kingdom, and which has, in reality, occasioned the present SUPPOSED Scarcity of Gold.

E R R A T A.

P. 10, l. 12 from bottom, for *either*, read *whether*
 25,— 6 from top, for *prepared*, read *proposed*
 28,— 3 from top, for (:) place (.)
 32,—10 from bottom, for *regu*, read *regular*
 33,— 7 from top, dele *regular and*
 40,— 8 from bottom, for (:) place (;)
 41,— 5 from top, for (.) place (:)
 —,—11 from ditto, for *fnrnish*, read *furnish*
 51,— 5 from bottom, for (:) place (;)
 —,— 3 from ditto, for (;) place (:)
 52,— 7 from top, for *became*, read *have become*

THE Projector of this great National Establishment, was a William Paterson, Esq. a Scotchman, who became one of the First Directors, and whose Name will be found in the List of the first Governors and Court of Directors, which will speedily follow. It was established for the support of Publick Credit, the prevention of extravagant Usury, and the utility of Trade in general, by Act of Parliament, in the 5th and 6th Years of the Reign of William and Mary ; which enacted, " That their Majesties by commission under the great Seal* might appoint Persons to take Subscriptions, on or before the first day of August, 1694, from any Persons, Natives, or Foreigners, for raising and paying into the Receipt

* The Commission here mentioned, was not, however, under the Great Seal, but by writ of Privy Seal, signed PIGOT, and bearing date, the 27th Day of July, in the Sixth Year of the above Reign.

B

of the Exchequer, 1,200,000l. for the security whereof, the Yearly sum of 140,000l. should be kept apart in the Receipt of the Exchequer, payable out of the Duties of Excise; out of which, the Yearly sum of 100,000l. should be applied to the use of the Subscribers. Their Majesties were also empowered to incorporate such Subscribers under the Name, or Title of THE GOVERNOR AND COMPANY OF THE BANK OF ENGLAND. The Restrictions upon them were, that they should not borrow more Money under their Common Seal, than the above sum of 1,200,000l. unless by Act of Parliament. That they should not with the Stock of the Company, trade by themselves, or suffer any Person in trust for them to trade in any sort of Goods or Merchandize whatsoever. But that they might deal in Bills of Exchange, and also in the buying and selling Bullion, Gold, or Silver; or in selling Goods Mortgaged to them, and not redeemed within three Months after the Time of such Redemption had expired. In consequence of the said Act, Books were

opened to receive Subscriptions at Exeter
Exchange in the Strand, on the 5th Day of
June, 1696; in which, the then Lords of
the Treasury subscribed 5000l. on the part of
his Majesty; but such was then the com-
plexion of the Times, that all the other Subscriptions taken together, amounted only to
2,100l. There were two reasons assigned for
this failure; the Friends of the Reigning
Monarch, attributed it to the machinations of
the JACOBITES; who, to do them Justice, had
made use of every means in their Power, to
prevent the Establishment; but the true Reason certainly was, that every kind of Security
both Publick and Private at that time, produced
an Interest of 8 per Cent. whereas these
shares only offered 5 : that this was the real
cause, the event shewed; for upon raising
the Interest to 8 per Cent. the Subscription
filled, and the Charter passed*. For this sum

* As it may be a matter of Curiosity to know
who were the First Governors and Directors, their Names are here set forth, Viz.

of 1,200,000l. the Corporation received an Annuity of 96,000l. being the Interest of the said sum at 8 per Cent. and 4000l. more per Annum for the Management, making in all 100,000l. per Annum, as before stated. In 1697, the Company were allowed to add to its Capital the further Sum of 1,001,171l. 10s. which then amounted to 2,201,171l. 10s. the

---

SIR JOHN HOUBLON, KNT. Governor.

MICHAEL GODFREY, ESQ. Deputy Governor.

DIRECTORS.

Sir John Huband, Bt.	Abr. Houblon, Esq.
Sir Jas. Houblon, Kt.	Gilbert Heathcote, Esq.
Sir William Gore, Kt.	Theodore Jansen, Esq.
Sir Wm. Scawen, Knt.	John Lordell, Esq.
Sir Hen. Furnese, Knt.	Sam. Lethieullier, Esq.
Sir Thos. Abney, Knt.	William Paterson, Esq.
Sir Wm. Hedges, Knt.	Robert Raworth, Esq.
Brook Bridges, Esq.	John Smith (Beaufort
James Bateman, Esq.	Buildings) Esq.
Geo. Boddington, Esq.	ObadiahSedgwick, Esq.
Edward Clerke, Esq	Nathaniel Tench, Esq.
James Denew, Esq.	John Ward, Esq.
Thos. Goddard, Esq.	

addition here mentioned, is said to have been for the support of Publick Credit ; this was probably the Fact, for in the preceding Year, Tallies had been at Forty, Fifty, and up to Sixty ; and the Company's own Notes to 20 per Cent. Discount ; this was during the great Recoinage of Silver, which took place at this time ; and the New Bank thinking it proper, for what reason was best known to themselves, to discontinue the payment of their Notes at the same period, the reason of their depression is easily accounted for. By the same Act which allowed the augmentation of their Capital, the Company's Stock was declared to be a personal, and not a real Estate ; and that it should be exempt from Taxes. That no Act of the Company should render the Stock liable to forfeiture ; but, that it should be subject to the Debts of the Company. That it should be Felony, without the benefit of Clergy, to forge the Company's Seal, or any sealed Bank Bill, or any Bank Note ; or to alter, or erase such Bills, or Notes.

In 1709, being the 7th of Queen Anne, they advanced a further sum of 400,000l. to Government; which being without Interest, reduced the Interest paid by Government upon the whole sum advanced to them; viz. 1,600,000l. to 6 per Cent. By the said Act they were empowered to encrease their Capital to 4,402,343l. and the Company to continue to the 1st of August, 1732. By another Act of the 9th of Anne, it was provided, That every Person being Governor, Deputy Governor, or Director, should for that Year be incapacitated from acting as a Director of the East India Company. The before recited Act of the 7th of Anne, was repealed in part, by an Act which passed in the 12th Year of the said Queen; which enacts, that upon 12 Months notice after the 1st of August, 1742, and upon the repayment of all the Sums due from Government to the Corporation, and all the Arrears of Interest due thereupon, the Company should cease and determine.

In 1714, the Company advanced to the Government another Loan of 1,000,000l. and 500,000l. and the term of their existence as a Corporation was prolonged to 1742.

In 1716, the 3d of George I. the Interest was reduced to 5 per Cent. and the Company agreed to deliver up 2,000,000l. of Exchequer Bills, and to accept an Annuity of 100,000l. payable out of the Agregate Fund, and the Duties upon Houses; and they were empowered by the same Act, whenever they should see cause, to call upon their Members for any sums of Money, which in a General Court should be judged necessary, in proportion to their respective interests in the Capital Stock.

In 1722, the Corporation purchased Four Millions of the South Sea Company's Capital Stock; to enable them to pay for which, they sold New Stock of their own to the amount of 3,389,831l. at 118 per Cent; with this Stock, so purchased from the South Sea Company, they received an adequate share of the allowance from Government for management, amounting to 1,898l. 3s. 5d.

In the Year 1725, the 12th of George I. the Bank agreed to reduce the interest upon the Two Millions of Exchequer Bills, given up in the Year 1716, from 5 to 4 per Cent. And in the Year 1727, they paid into the Exchequer the Sum of 1,750,000l. for which they were to receive 70,000l. per Annum, subject to redemption, and payable out of the Duties upon Coal and Culm.

In the Year 1728, they advanced to Government 1,250,000l. for an Annuity of 50,000l. payable out of the additional Duties upon Soap, Paper, Stamp Duties, &c. all of which had been before mortgaged to the South Sea Company. In this Year the Government paid to the Bank 500,000l. on Account, for the Two Millions of Exchequer Bills given up in 1716; and in 1737, the further Sum of One Million for the same purpose, which reduced that Debt from Two Millions to 500,000l. as also the whole Debt due from Government to the Company, to 1,600,000l. The Charter of incorporation expiring in the Year 1742, the Company obtained a renewal, or rather extension of it to the Year 1764, for which they engaged to advance to Government 1,600,000l. at 3 per Cent. They were enabled by the Act which passed upon this occasion, to add the said Sum to their Capital, which was thereby now encreased to 3,200,000l. the one Half bearing Interest at 4, and the other Half at 3 per Cent. And the same Act declares, that no other Bank shall be allowed by Parliament, nor that any Body Politick or Corporate, or any other Persons whatever, united in Partnership, above the number of Six, throughout England, should borrow, or take up any sums of Money upon their Notes payable at less time than Six Months, during the continuance of such privilege to this Company: this Act also declared them a Corporation, for exclusive Banking, above the number of Six, as before

recited, but subjected the same to Redemption
upon one Year's Notice, after the first Day of
August, 1764, upon repayment of their Principal, Interest, and all arrears of Annuity
up to that time by Government. We come
now to a Memorable Epocha, in the History
of this incorporated Company, viz. the Year
1745, in which the similarity of circumstances
with the present Time, *appears* very striking;
but though the Effects have been nearly the
same, the Causes are widely different: in
1745, an Invasion *had absolutely taken Place,*
and the Enemy (no matter either Foreign
or Domestic) were in full march to the Capital. They had defeated the Troops sent
against them by Government; encouraged
and enriched by their depredations, they were
advancing with hasty strides to the Metropolis,
and had reached the heart of the Kingdom:
here was real room for Fear to enter the ima-
gination, and a *real Danger* to be apprehended;
for although it may be said that they were too
few to carry their original intention of de-
throning the reigning Monarch into execution,

yet they were powerful enough to have done great mischief; and their arrival at London was not at all problematical, had they come on, instead of retreating, when we consider their Courage and Ferocity, together with the few Regular Troops then in the Kingdom to oppose them: from Derby (where the Rebels arrived on the 4th and 5th of December) to London, is but 117 Miles; which would not have taken much more than Three Days to accomplish, and at which latter place, the Friends and Adherents of the Young Adventurer had proceeded so far, as to print his Declaration, and disperse them all over the Capital, by dropping them in the Streets, putting them under the Doors, &c. &c. &c. But to proceed: for some Days previous to the 26th of September in this Year, a Run upon the Bank had taken place, which threatened the draining it of all the Specie therein, and which the Corporation endeavoured to procrastinate as much as possible, by making all their payments in Silver; more especially Sixpences; but on that Day a meeting of the

Principal Merchants, Traders, and Bankers, took place; in which the following Resolution was entered into, and signed by upwards of 1100 Names. " We the undersigned Mer-" chants and others being sensible how ne-" cessary the preservation of Publick Credit is " at this Time, do hereby declare, that we " will not refuse to receive Bank Notes in " payment of any Sum of Money to be paid " to us; and we will use our utmoſt endea-" vours, to make all our payments in the same " manner." This Measure had the desired effect, the Run ceased, and Bank Notes circulated, with as much ease and Credit as before. On the 20th of January, 1746, the Corporation at a General Court held that Day, came to the Resolution of empowering their Directors to lend the Government One Million at Four per Cent. to be secured on the Malt and Land Tax: and also to subscribe One Thousand Pounds to the Scheme, for the Relief, Support, and Encouragement of the Soldiery. The Act for establishing the above Loan, received the Royal Assent on

Thursday, the 13th of February following. On the 11th of March, at a General Court, the Dividend was declared to be 2¾ per Cent. on their Capital Stock, for the half Year, ending on the 25th Day ensuing; and they deferred the call for the second payment on their Capital, which was to be made on the 28th, to the 7th of April. And on the 18th of September, at another General Court, the Dividend declared for the half Year ending at Michaelmas, was 2¾ per Cent. as before. In this Year also, the Government I suppose not being able to discharge the Sum of 986,800l. due to the Company on Exchequer Bills, unsatisfied by the Duties for licensing the selling of Spirits by retail; the Corporation cancelled the same, and received an Annuity instead, of 39,472l. being the Interest at 4 per Cent. on the above Sum: and they were permitted to add the former Sum to their Capital.

In 1747, the Dividends declared in that Year on their Capital Stock, was at the rate

C

of $2\frac{1}{2}$ per Cent. on each of their Half Yearly Payments for the first time, of its being reduced so low. At a General Court held at Merchants Taylors Hall, Jan. 31st, 1750, a Resolution was passed by a great Majority, not to agree to an Act which had passed that Sessions of Parliament, for reducing the Annuities bearing 4 per Cent. to the several Rates contained therein. At another General Court held Jan. 2d, 1752, it was agreed to lend the Government 1,400,000l. to be repaid out of the Sinking Fund; and at a further General Court, held on the 21st Day of September, this Year, the Dividend was declared to be $2\frac{1}{2}$ per Cent. as for the preceding half Year; but the Proprietors were informed that in future their Dividends could not be so much: and accordingly the next Dividend declared, at a General Court, held March 15th, 1753, was only $2\frac{1}{4}$ per Cent.

In 1759, the Corporation gave Notice in April, that they would in future issue their Notes for the several Sums of Fifteen, and

Ten Pounds each, none before that time having been circulated for less Sums than Twenty.

In 1763, (as their Charter was to expire in
1764) an Act passed ;* by the Tenth Clause
of which it is enacted, That the Corporation
shall pay into the receipt of the Exchequer,
for his Majesty's use, the Sum of 110,000l.
on or before the 23d Day of April, 1764 :
and that they shall not be entitled to the repayment of the Principal, or be allowed any Interest for the same; and the next Clause (11th)
declares them a Body Corporate and Politic
for ever, with all the Immunities, Privileges,
&c. &c. granted before to them by all the Acts
which had passed in the Reigns of William
and Mary, Anne, and George II. but although this Clause declares as aforesaid, yet
the next Clause, viz. 12th, is a Clause of
Redemption ; which, if I understand it aright,

* See Ruffhead's Statutes at Large, Vol. 9,
Fol. 183, being the 4th of Geo. III. Cap. 25.

subjected them to a further renewal of their Charter in the Year 1786, but whether with respect to their ceasing to be a Corporation altogether, or whether it only extended to their Privilege of Exclusive Banking, and to the extinguishing of their original Annuity of 96,000l. and 4000l. more for management, as granted to them by their Charter of Incorporation in 1694, I am not *Lawyer* enough to determine; however, as that Year (1786) went over without the required Notice being given, or any Act passed, relative to them, it may be said that they are, as before recited, " A Body Corporate and Politic for ever."

In 1788, at a General Court held on the 19th day of March, the Interest upon their Capital Stock was declared to be at the rate of 7 per Cent. per Annum; at which rate it still continues. Not any thing very material has happened since, until Feb. 26th, 1797, when a Minute was entered at a Privy Council held that Day, as follows:

At the Council Chamber, Whitehall,
Feb. 26th, 1797.

By the Lords of His Majesty's
Most Hon. Privy Council.

PRESENT.

The Lord Chancellor.
Lord President.
Duke of Portland.
Marquis Cornwallis.
Earl Spencer.
Earl of Liverpool.
Lord Grenville.
Mr. Chancellor of the Exchequer.

" Upon the representation of the Chancellor of the Exchequer, stating, that from the result of the Information which he has received, and of the enquiries which it has been his duty to make respecting the effect of the unusual Demands for Specie that have been made upon the Metropolis, in consequence of

C 3

ill-founded or exaggerated Alarms in different parts of the Country, it appears, that unless some Measure is immediately taken, there may be reason to apprehend a want of a sufficient supply of Cash to answer the exigencies of the publick service : it is the unanimous opinion of the Board, that it is indispensably necessary for the publick Service, that the Directors of the Bank of England should forbear issuing any Cash in payment, until the sense of Parliament can be taken on that subject, and the proper measures adopted thereupon, for maintaining the means of circulation, and supporting the publick and commercial credit of the Kingdom at this important conjuncture ; and it is ordered that a Copy of this Minute be transmitted to the Directors of the Bank of England, and they are hereby required, on the grounds of the exigency of the case, to conform thereto, until the sense of Parliament can be taken as aforesaid.

        (Signed)   W. FAWKENER."

In consequence of this Order, the Bank delivered Papers on Monday Feb. 27th : conta...ing the said Minute of Council, and also the following Address to their Proprietors and the Publick:

"*Bank of England, Feb. 27th. 1797.*

" The Governor, Deputy Governor, and Directors of the Bank of England, think it their Duty to inform the Proprietors of Bank Stock, as well as the publick at large, that the general concerns of the Bank, are in the most affluent, and prosperous situation; and such as to preclude every doubt as to the security of its Notes. The Directors mean to continue their usual Discounts for the accomodation of the commercial interest, paying the amount in Bank Notes, and the Dividend Warrants will be paid in the same manner.

FRANCIS MARTIN, *Secretary.*"

The circulation of these Papers, occasioned (as might reasonably be expected), a great Alarm: equal if not superior to what was felt during the Rebellion in the Year 1745, when the Enemy was so near London. Measures were immediately adopted to allay the ferment.

A most respectable Meeting of the first Merchants, Bankers, and Traders in the Metropolis, was held at the Mansion House, on the same Day, when the following Resolution was entered into, and signed by all present :

" *MANSION HOUSE*, LONDON,
Feb. 27*th* 1797.

" At a Meeting of Merchants, Bankers &c. held here this Day, to consider of the Steps which it may be proper to take, to prevent embarassments to publick Credit, from the effect of any ill-founded or exaggerated Alarms ; and to support it with the utmost exertions at the present important conjuncture. The Lord Mayor in the Chair.

" Resolved unanimously,

" That we the undersigned, being highly sensible how necessary the preservation of publick Credit is at this time, do most readily hereby declare, that we will not refuse to receive Bank Notes in Payment of any Sum of Money to be paid to us ; and we will use our utmost endeavours to make all our payments in the same manner."

This Resolution having remained for some few Days, was found to have received between Three, and Four Thousand Signatures.

On Tuesday Feb. 28th, on the Motion of the Chancellor of the Exchequer in the House of Commons, a Secret Committee was appointed to examine the Accompts of the Bank, &c. and on the 3d Day of March following, they presented the following Report to the House :

" The Committee appointed to examine and state the total amount of outstanding Demands on the Bank of England, and likewise of the Funds for discharging the same, and to report the result thereof to the House, together with their opinion on the necessity of providing for the confirmation and continuance, for a time to be limited, of measures taken in pursuance of the Minute of Council on the 26th of February last, and who are empowered to report their proceedings from time to time, to the House; have pursuant to an Order of the House, proceeded to examine into the several matters referred to their consideration, and have unanimously agreed upon the following Report, viz.

" Your Committee have examined the total amount of outstanding Demands on the Bank of England, and likewife of the Funds for difcharging the fame : and think it their duty without lofs of time, to ftate thofe total amounts, and to report the refult thereof to the House.

" Your Committee find upon such examination, that the total amount of outstanding Demands on the Bank, on the 25th Day of February last (to which Day the Accounts could be compleatly made up) was 13,770,390l. and that the total amount of the Funds for discharging those Demands (not including the

permanent Debt due from Government, of
11,686,800l. which bears an interest of 3 per
Cent.) was, on the same 25th Day of Feb.
last, 17,597,280l. AND THAT THE RESULT
IS, THAT THERE WAS ON THE 25TH DAY
OF FEB. LAST, A SURPLUS OF EFFECTS
BELONGING TO THE BANK BEYOND THE
AMOUNT OF THEIR DEBTS, AMOUNTING TO
THE SUM OF 3,826,890l. EXCLUSIVE OF
THE ABOVE-MENTIONED PERMANENT DEBT
OF 11,686,800l. DUE FROM GOVERNMENT.

" And your Committee further represent,
that since the 25th of Feb. last, considerable
issues have been made by the Bank, in Bank
Notes, both upon Government Securities, and
in discounting Bills, the particulars of which
could not immediately be made up; but as
those issues appear to your Committee to have
been made upon corresponding Securities,
taken with the usual care and attention, the
actual balance in favour of the Bank did not
appear to your Committee to have been thereby
diminished."

On the representation of the Bankers, &c.
not only to the Directors, but also to Mr.
Pitt, the Corporation came to the determina-
tion of issuing small Notes of One, and Two
Pounds each, in exchange for larger ones,
and in a few Days thereafter appeared the
following Advertisement :

    " *Bank of England, March 6th,* 1797.

    " *In order to accommodate the Publick with
a further supply of Coin for small payments,* a
quantity of Dollars which have been supplied
by the Bank, and stamped at the Mint, are
now ready to be issued at the Bank, at the
price of 4s. 6d. per Dollar ; *and a further
quantity is preparing.*"

But although this Advertisement appeared,
the Dollars were not put in circulation agreea-
ble thereto ; it having been suggested that the
price put upon them was too small, being
nearly 2d. under their real value : therefore
three Days after appeared the following :

" *Bank of England, March 9th,* 1797.

" *In consequence of its appearing to be the general opinion, that the Dollars will be more conveniently circulated at the rate of* 4s. 9d. *per Dollar, than at that of* 4s. 6d. *which had been prepared, Notice is hereby given,* that Dollars are now ready to be delivered accordingly, at the rate of Four Shillings and Ninepence per Dollar."

And they were issued in consequence; so great was the application while the *Mania of Alarm* was at its height, that the Hall at the Bank was crowded Day after Day repeatedly, to obtain *some value* for that Paper, which the Enemies of the Ministry, in all places, had endeavoured to depress. However, the first Report of the Secret Committee to the House of Commons, had, in great measure, allayed the ferment, and although every means was employed by the Gentlemen in Opposition to explain away the sense of it, as much as possible, yet it had made by much too deep an impression to be easily effaced by all

D

the sophistry made use of upon that occasion; the consequence was, that although at first you was obliged to wait hours before it became your turn to be served with the Dollars, as the people stood ten or twelve deep at the Tellers Counters; yet when the before-mentioned Report of the Committee came to be coolly considered, and that although the demand for them was great, and for the first few Days seemingly increasing, yet as there appeared no want, but every one was supplied as fast as possible; such is the versatility of the human mind, that thereafter, it sensibly decreased every Day, and in less than a Month from their first issue, any one might walk in, and obtain his Five Pounds worth, with very little trouble.

I have thus brought this little History down to the time present, and have only now to add, that the profits of this Corporation arises from their traffic in Bullion; the discounting of Bills of Exchange; and the Cash they receive from Government for managing the Publick Funds, also from the Money allowed for the circu-

lation of Exchequer Bills, and for receiving
the Subscriptions for Loans and Lotteries:
the allowance for managing the Publick Funds
was, previous to 1786, 562l. 10s. per Million, but in that Year it was reduced to 450l.
per Million; for receiving Subscriptions to
Loans, 805l. 15s. 10d. per Million; and for
Lotteries generally 1000l. for the whole; but
these two last Articles have varied, according
to the number of Subscribers to the one, or
Tickets in the other. In 1772, 1774, and
1775, the allowance for the Lotteries in those
Years, were 2000l. each; as being connected
with the Loans, they were attended with
more than ordinary trouble. All these items
together with the Interest paid by *Government
on their capital*, form a Fund, sufficient to di-
vide 7 per Cent. to the several Proprietors of
that part of their Capital Stock, on which Dividends are, paid which at this time amounts
to 11,642,400l.

Having thus traced this great, opulent, and
useful Corporation, from its establishment to
the present time, it will be necessary to make

some remarks, contrast their situations at different times, and from those inferences, draw some general conclusions : it must have been observed they had great difficulties to struggle with at their first outset,* the whole Body of the JACOBITES, and they were by no means to be despised for want either of weight, or influence ; if my Readers consult the Historians of that Day, they will find, that many great People were in the interest of the abdicated Family, and whoever dips into Dalrymple's Annals of that Time, will find who they were ; they have likewise survived two Rebellions, and any one who has perused the preceding pages with the smallest degree of Attention, cannot but be struck with the great similitude between the latter end of the Year

---

* April 24, 1694. Dissentient. Against that part of the Bill, which relates to the incorporating the Governor and Company of the Bank of England, and the Clauses that concern the same.

Aylesbury,	Winchelsea,	Montague,
Rochester,	Sandwich,	Nottingham,
Essex,	Thos. Roffen,	

No Reasons assigned, as it appears.

1745, and the present Time; at both periods nearly the same methods were pursued; the run upon the Corporation for Specie was the same, and the same methods were adopted to support its Credit, with this difference, as to situation: that, in 1745, the numbers who subscribed their Names to the Association for circulating Bank Notes, were only about 1100, and now nearly Four Thousand. At that time, a daring and ferocious Enemy, as before stated, was within three Days march of the Capital, and which, had not Providence interfered, to distract their Councils, *they certainly might have reached.* *An Invasion from France* in support of the Pretender, was by far more probable, than at present: a large Force was assembled upon their Coast, under some of their most experienced Generals; all the small Craft collected in great Bodies, for the conveyance of Stores, &c. and above all, a Fleet *equal, if not superior to our own* ; nay, so much did our Government expect them to put their Threats into execution, that Alarm Posts were fixed upon for the Troops to repair to, upon Signal given, which, in London and Westminster, was to be the firing a Cannon every half minute, to the number of 7 ; if at the Tower, to be answered immediately by those in St. James's Park ; and if first in the Park, to be answered by those at the Tower ; upon hearing which, the London Militia then on Duty, with other Corps, were to repair immediately to their Alarm Posts, without beat of Drum ; and the same Proclamation strictly charged and commanded, that no Ship in the River should discharge any Cannon, Swivel, or any large Fire Arms, under a heavy Punishment ; and to shew that this was the Fact, I shall here insert a Letter, wrote by the celebrated Admiral Vernon, at that time Commander in the Downs.

> *Norwich, in the Downs,*
> *Dec.* 20, 1745.

Sir,

" *From the Intelligence I have procured last Night, of the Enemy having brought away from*

Dunkirk, great numbers of their small Embark-
ations, and many of them laden with Cannon,
Field Carriages, Powder, Shot, and other
Military Stores; the Irish Troops also being
marched out of Dunkirk towards Calais, General Lowendahl and many other Officers being
at Dunkirk, with a young Person among them
they call the Prince, and who was said to be the
second Son of the Pretender; as I can't but
apprehend they are preparing for a Descent from
the Ports of Calais and Boulogne, and which I
suspect may be attempted at Dungeness, where
many of my Cruizers are in motion for; and I
have some thoughts of my moving To-morrow
with part of my Ships, if the Weather should be
moderate for a Descent; I thought it my duty
for his Majesty's service to advise you of it,
and to desire you will communicate this my Letter
to the Mayor of Deal, and that the neighbouring
Towns should have advice for assembling for
their common Defence; that my Cruizers signals
for discovering the approach of an Enemy, will
be their Jack Flag, flying at their Top-mast

Head, and firing a Gun every half hour, and to desire they will forward the alarm.

To John Norris, Esq.
at Deal Castle, or to
the Mayor of Deal in
his Absence.

I am, Sir,
Your humble Servant,
E. VERNON.

At this time too, be it remembered, that the Company had not *submitted their affairs to inspection*; and the whole of the Regular Troops, for the protection of all the Counties next the Channel, viz. Norfolk, Essex, Kent, Sussex, and Hampshire, did not exceed Ten Thousand Men, Horse and Foot included, and we had at that time no regular Militia. The contrast to all this at the present Time is striking: we have now no Rebellion at Home to disturb and distract us; a more powerful Fleet than ever we were possessed of before; that of our Enemy almost annihilated; thus Masters of the Seas, how are they to come? This same Fleet of ours, commanded by Men of tried and approved Courage, which was not the case in

1745; no Alarm Posts now fixed; no Proclamations about Signals; no Army at present upon the opposite Coast, at least, in no great numbers; added to all which, the Regular Troops in the County of Essex alone, are more than was then distributed in the beforementioned Five, besides a regular and well disciplined Militia of One Hundred Thousand Men, exclusive of the regulars; and without taking into the Account, the Fencible and Yeomanry Cavalry, and the Volunteer Corps; when all this comes to be maturely weighed and considered, let the most timorous ask himself, from whence arises the fear of an *Invasion?* and its consequent effect, the run upon the Bank, who have also, which I had almost forgotten to mention, *had their accounts inspected,* as before seen; the *report upon which,* OUGHT TO SILENCE EVERY BABLER, AND DISPEL EVERY FEAR. By casting a retrospective view also, over the preceding Narrative, it will likewise appear, that the Bank has at all times, from the instant of their incorporation, assisted the Government with Cash: which some of the Gentlemen in

Opposition, more remarkable for the *flippancy of their wit, than the soundness of their judgement,* would wish to have understood as a new measure ; but what will be said, when it is stated, that one of the Directors now in Parliament, in a debate which took place, March 27th, upon the reading of the Bank Indemnity Bill, afferted in his speech, that even in the administration of Mr. Fox, the Government was then indebted to the Bank for Cash advanced, 10,300,000l. and by a Paper which now lays before me, signed Abraham. Newland, which was ordered to be printed for the use of the Members of the House of Commons, March 7th, 1797, it is stated, that there is outstanding and due to this Corporation, for Money advanced up to Decr. 25th, 1796, the Sum of 10,847,568l. 13s. 7d,* which is only 547,568l. 13s 7d. more then was advanced to the great leader of the opposition ; whence

---

* *Bank of England, March 4th, 1797.* An Account of the Money advanced by the Bank of England, for the Publick Service, and outstanding on the 25th Decr. 1796.

then this great outcry against the present
Ministry? except for the purposes of party: to
mislead the unwary, and at all events to force
them out of power, in order to possess their
places. If we consider the Minute of Council,
which gave rise to all this confusion, will it not

			£.	s.	d.
On Land Tax	1794	141,000			
Ditto	1795	369,000			
Ditto	1796	1,757,000			
Ditto	1797	2,000,000			
		4,267,000			
Malt	1794	196,000			
Ditto	1795	172,000			
Ditto	1796	750,000			
Ditto	1797	750,000			
		1,868,000			
Conolidated Fund	1795	1,054,000			
Ditto	1796	1,323,000			
Vote of Credit for 2,500,000l.	1796	821,400			
		3,198,400			
Exchequer Bills without Interest		376,739	0	9	
		9,710,139	0	9	
Treasury Bills of Exchange		1,137,429	12	10	
		10,847,568	13	7	

be found to originate in the people themſelves ? it was their unfounded fear : more eſpecially in the country, and again in Scotland and Ireland, which occaſioned them to make their demands *all at once* upon the Country Banks : these had made their deposits with the London Bankers, and thoſe again with the Bank of England ; thus the first being drawn upon, affected the whole : and I much queſtion, if there had not been so many Country Banks, whether this call for Specie would have ever reached the Metropolis ; but I shall enlarge upon the probable causes, which in my opinion was the real and substantial occaſion, of the scarcity of Spécie, when I come to treat upon the Coin and Bullion, which as one of the branches of trade to which the Company is confined ; this little Work would not be compleat without doing ; and to which I ſhall immediately direct my Attention without fur- ther Preface.

On METALS and COIN.

When the inconvenience of bartering one commodity for another occured, the human Mind, ever active, employed itself, no doubt, to find out a substitute, which should answer all those purposes ; it is no wonder that Metals, from their compactness, durability, and the easiness by which their parts might be disunited, and again joined by fusion, or other means, should be adopted for that purpose ; and we find, that it was so : Iron, was in common use among the Spartans ; Copper, more general than any other Metal, among the Romans ; and until the time of Servius Tullius, if we are to believe Pliny, who asserts it in his Natural History, Lib. 33, Cap. 3, (upon the authority of a more ancient Historian than himself,) they had no Coined Money, but made use of the Metals in rough bars. But this method

E

although an improvement, was not yet compleat : being attended with great difficulty and
trouble, especially in the finer Metals of Gold
and Silver, which were not only to be weigh·
ed with great exactness, but was subject to
adulteration, to the great dimunition of their
real value, and which could only be detected
by Assaying or Hydrostaticks; neither of which
were discovered at that time ; but if they had
been in use, both processes were by much too
troublesome, to be of any service in the common intercourse between mankind : to remedy
these inconveniences, the Stamping certain
portions, accurately weighed, of the different
Metals, with various devices, under the sanction
of the Governments who were virtually pledged
for the truth, both of the weight and fineness of
the various portions of the Metals so stamped,
was undoubtedly the origin of the present
Coin ; but then it must be remembered, that
the weight, and the name of the Coin corres-
ponded : thus the Pound Sterling, in the Reign
of Edward I. contained one pound of Silver,

whose fineness was known and ascertained. The Tower pound, was at that time something less than the present pound Troy; this last weight was not introduced into the English Mint, till the time of Henry VIII. The name Troy weight now used, was antiently Troyes weight being made use of, at the great Mart, or Fair of Troyes in Champagne, which in the Reign of Charlemagne, was greatly resorted to by all the nations of Europe, and therefore the dissemination of its weights, measures, customs, &c. are easily accounted for. The Livre of France contained at this time also, one pound of Silver, Troyes weight, and the Pennies of England, France, Scotland, &c. were each of them one Pennyweight of Silver of the same fineness with the pound; so that at that period as well as at this, the Penny was the 240th part of the Pound Sterling. But although there was this uniformity between the parts of the Penny, and the Pound, it was not so with the intermediate Silver Coins: thus the Shilling among our Saxon ancestors, at one time, contained only

5 Pennies: and it was still more variable among our neighbours the French: for with them at different times, the Shilling contained 5, 12, 20, and sometimes 40 Pennies. This was however during the times of the first Kings of France; but from the Reign of Charlemagne in France, and William the Conqueror in England, the relative proportion between the Penny, the Shilling, and the Pound, seems to have been pretty well established, as it now remains. However we may have preserved the names, the substance seems to have nearly escaped us; thus the value of the ounce of Silver at the time before specified, was only 20 Pence, or Pennies, whereas it is now more than three times dearer: and therefore our Pound Sterling now, does not contain quite one third of its original value, or rather weight.

Dr. Smith in his excellent Book on the Wealth of Nations, attributes this generally to " the avarice and injustice of Princes, and Sovereign States, abusing the confidence

of their subjects ;" I do not agree with him,
unless it can be proved, that those Princes, &c.
procured the Metals, at the old original Prices,
and after stamping or coining them, circulated
them at the new. That this is not the case,
every one conversant, or indeed who barely
knows the price of Gold or Silver, in an un-
wrought state, can testify ; thus in my opinion,
the fault attaches not to the Princes and
Sovereign States, as Dr. Smith would have
it, but to those who furnish the Metals to
them ; who again are governed by the current
price affixed to them, by the scarcity, or
plenty, occasioned by the exchange being for,
or against the country, who has need of
them at that time. To keep as much of these
precious Metals in any Kingdom or State, has
I believe been pretty generally the case of
all Governments ; hence arise the many laws
against their exportation, especially when coined ; yet let these laws, however rigorous, be
once put in competition, with the interest of
the Merchant or Trader, and their effect will
be found of little consequence ; although they

may not always run the risque of exporting it, in its coined state, yet a Crucible, and an Ingot Mould, will always furnish them with the means of so doing.—In the Mercantile Language, Gold and Silver are commodities equally to be exported and imported, as any other Metal, or Merchandize whatever; I will grant thus much, confining it to the rough state, or to foreign Coin; but when once it has received the impression of the Die of Coinage, from that moment I look upon it as the certain and absolute property of that State, whose distinguishing device it bears, and a certain degree of criminality attaches to every one concerned in its transportation from such State, but in a much greater degree to that Person who is a natural Subject of it.

It might be a matter of curious speculation, to enquire why Gold has been more plentiful in this Kingdom, than in any other Nation, or State, however large, upon the Continent, Portugal excepted; and yet such is the fact: in Germany, France, Spain, Italy, &c. the

Circulating Medium, to make use of a fashionable phrase, is almost universally Silver; here the direct contrary; for till very lately that the issuing of Dollars from the Bank took place, it was scarcely possible to procure Silver, in exchange for *one* Guinea, much more in larger Sums; and instances have occurred, within my own knowledge, where 2, 3, and 4 per Cent. has been given for a quantity of Silver above One Hundred Pounds worth. When we consider that, upon a fair average of seven Years, the Importation of Gold and Silver to the two great Emporiums for those Metals, Cadiz and Lisbon, amounts only to about 6,000,000l. per Annum, including both the registered and the smuggled, it becomes matter of surprize, how all the Nations of Europe are supplied, even to the quantity they have, with current Coin; the more so, when we consider the quantity of both, which are annually made use of in those Manufactures, where there cannot be even a hope of their revivification, if I may be allowed the expression; for instance, the Plating Business, at the

Town of Birmingham alone, is supposed to consume 50,000l. sterling per Annum; and it must be allowed, that Silver or Gold so employed, can never be renovated; and the Gold expended in the gilding of Books, Furniture, the inferior Metals, &c. &c. &c. although it may appear trifling upon the first view, yet upon consideration of the extent of such use, and when added thereto, that it never can be regained, it will be found to amount to much more than could be expected. If the consumption of Birmingham alone before stated, to be 50,000l. which is equal to 120th part of the whole; I think we may readily conclude, that with the assistance of all the rest of the Nations who make use of those Metals, that the expenditure at least equals the supply. It is a curious fact, related by the before-mentioned Dr. Smith, " that Gold was not considered as a legal Tender for a long time after it was coined into Money." This shews that there was a time, when this universal idol, the stopping the circulation of which, is now so deplored,

and bewailed, could not, without a previous
Agreement, protect a Man from Imprisonment,
nor save him from a merciless Creditor, although his House was filled with it.   But I
must hasten to the point, to which all that I
have hitherto said upon the subject, has been
preliminary ; and that is, To what is the present scarcity of circulating *Gold* to be attributed? The opposition to the present Ministry,
in both the Houses of Parliament, will, and
do tell you daily, over and over again, and in
the *same Words too, in both Houses,* and which
they have repeated for some time past, that it
is owing to the War ; and more particularly to
the remittances which have been made to our
Ally the Emperor ; if I thought them *serious*
in those assertions, I should pity their want of
knowledge, and endeavour to ENLIGHTEN
them ; but as I consider all that they say upon
that Head, mere matter of course, and pro-
ceeding from the same Cause, which has in-
spired every Opposition in the British Parliament, since Oppositions were known there,
viz. a desire to *get in,* and replace those,

whom they wish to *turn out*; I shall leave them therefore to themselves, and for the information of those, who, like myself, are of no party, endeavour to shew, that the present scarcity of Gold Coin, *if indeed there is a scarcity*, which, I much doubt, proceeds from other causes, though the effect may be the same. To meet the assertion, that it proceeds from our Remittances to the Emperor, I will oppose another assertion, equally bold perhaps, but fortunately more true ; and that is, HAD ALL THE REMITTANCES TO THE EMPEROR BEEN MADE IN SPECIE, AND THAT SPECIE, GOLD, IT WOULD NOT HAVE AMOUNTED TO ABOVE ONE-TENTH PART OF THAT METAL COINED IN THIS REIGN ALONE. But it is a notorious fact, of which the Opposition could not be ignorant, that most of those Remittances were made by Bills of Exchange, and if any Specie, it was generally, if not always, in Silver. But let us turn our eyes from misstators, and endeavour to find out the real drains for the Specie in Circulation : in the first place, as I have before stated, whenever

the Merchant finds it to his advantage, to export Bullion, either Gold or Silver, he will
certainly do it, as he looks upon them merely
as much the object of Mercantile Speculation,
as any other Commodity; and I firmly believe, that whenever there was an issue of new
Guineas from the Bank, that many thousands
of them almost immediately found their way
to Holland, Flanders, aud France; and I was
at one time credibly informed, that not a
Packet sailed for either the former or the latter of those places, but the former more especially, that did not convey some Thousands
every trip, the profit upon each Guinea, as
then stated, was very trifling; if I remember
right, about 3½d. or 4d. If so small a temp-
tation could operate, what are we to suppose
was the case, when, but a short time before
the Minute of Council stopped the issue of
Specie from the Bank, the English Guinea
was asserted to be worth at Hamburgh
1l. 5s. 3d. The American War also diminished the Guineas in circulation very much;
many, very many, indeed, were sent there,

which never found their way back. The
Congress took an effectual method to prevent
that; for whenever a Guinea got into their
hands, a piece, very near $\frac{1}{4}$ of it, was cut out,
and it was then sent again into circulation at
its original value of 21 Shillings. If added to
all this, the depredations committed upon
them, especially the new ones, at all times by
the small workers in Gold, who condemned
them without mercy to the crucible, all over the
kingdom, together with the 3,000,000l. for the
purchase of Coin, during the scarcity lately
experienced, and also the quantity sent to Ireland, in the course of every year, I think we
have no need to look to the Emperor, as the
great cause of their deficiency.

THE REMEDY.

The only way in my opinion to cure the
evils here stated, and to keep our Coin in this
Kingdom, is to make the difference between
its nominal, and real value, so much, as to
prevent its being melted at home, or exported
abroad, was it to be so, if at any time the

exigencies of the State, should even oblige the
Government themselves to export it, as was
the case, I believe in the American War, to
pay the Troops; yet from its not being so valua-
ble any where but here, it would to a certainty
find its way back again ; and that this would
be so, is sufficiently apparent at present ; since
those very Guineas recently exported clan-
destinely to Hamburgh, are (on account of the
Exchange having risen considerably in favour
of England since that time) now coming
back again in large quantities : and that the
Exchange has so risen in our favour, is to
be attributed, to that Report of the Committee
of both Houses of Parliament, appointed to
inspect the affairs of the Bank ; which
Report, redounds so much to the HONOUR,
STABILITY, AND FLOURISHING CONDITION
OF THAT GREAT AND OPULENT CORPO-
RATION.

I shall now proceed to the other great
Branch of the Company's Trade ; viz. the
Discounting of Bills.

F

NOTES, AND BILLS OF EXCHANGE.

Two sorts of Money, or mediums of Traffic are now extant; the one real, the other ideal: of the former I have spoke, in the preceding observations upon Metals and Coin; and on the latter, I here mean to say a few words. When Commerce, or Barter, for although their names differ, they are *essentially* the same; had arisen to that height, as to preclude the first measure of *really* exchanging one commodity for the other, by the intervention of Metals and Coin, still as these were found to be extremely troublesome as well as danger-ous, to remove, to any great distance, the medium of Letters, or Bills of Exchange, was invented to obviate those difficulties.*

* Bills of Exchange were first mentioned in Henry IId's time, Anno 1160; but not used

Without going at all into the niceties of
Exchange, as whether it is more advantageous
to remit Bullion, or to draw Bills upon any
given place, it will be sufficient for the present
purpose, shortly to explain what was at first
the real intention of them : it was certainly to
facilitate Commerce, inasmuch as I can convey to the most distant part of the Globe, with
which my then place of residence is anyways
commercially connected, as much Money in
one small Letter, to be paid to myself if
I intended to go there personally, or to any
one else, whom I might chuse to send,
as would take many Horses and Carriages
to convey : provided I either took it with me,
or sent it in Specie, not to mention the time
which would be lost by the latter method ; by
the same means, I can pay a Debt, or convey
Money to a person at any part of the commer-

---

in England, until 1307, 1st Year of Edward
II. And in 1381, the 5th of Richard II.
they were the only mode allowed of by law
for sending Money out of the Kingdom.

cial world, without stirring from home, or running the risque of sending it in Cash ; such was certainly the real origin of the subject now under discussion ; but however laudable and useful in their first state, they like all other human inventions, however excellent, became subject to misuse.

Postlethwayt in his Dictionary of Trade and Commerce, mentions four kinds of Exchanges, viz. Common Exchange, Real Exchange, *Dry Exchange, and Fictitious Exchange* ; of which the two latter were *usurious*, and were prohibited by the 3d, and 4th of Henry VII. He also pronounces this exordium in their favour :

" Foreign Bills of Exchange have long been looked on as the most obligatory, and convenient paper security, that is amongst Merchants ; not so much by virtue of the laws of any Country, as in conformity to the universal customs, and usages established amongst traders themselves, by a kind of una-

nimous concurrence for the facilitating a general Commerce throughout the World;" and
I find that he is also of my opinion with respect to their origin, although he carries it much
deeper into Antiquity, for he says,

" By the Romans, it is supposed to be in
use upwards of Two Thousand Years, Money
being then made out of Gold and Silver, to
avoid the Carriage of Merchandizes in Barter
from one Country to another: so other Nations, imitating the Jews and Romans, erected
Mints, and coined Monies, upon which the
Exchange by Bills was devised, *not only to
avoid the danger of the adventure of Monies, but
its troublesome Carriage.*" Mr. Rolt, in his
Dictionary of Trade and Commerce, published
in 1761, attributes their origin to a much later
time, and another cause, his Words are,

" A Bill of Exchange is a short Note or
Writing, ordering the payment of a sum of
Money in one place, to some Person assigned
by the Drawer or Remitter, in consideration

F 3

of the like value paid to him in another place, and in these Bills of Exchange, the whole Estate and Effects of Merchants usually consist, of which the skilful Negotiator makes a considerable profit. Bills of Exchange were unknown in the ancient Roman Commerce, as well as jurisprudence, and according to the common opinion, they are the invention of the Jews, who being banished from France, retired into Lombardy, about the twelfth Century, and found means, by the assistance of Merchants and Travellers, to withdraw their Effects, which they had lodged in the hands of Friends, by secret Letters and Bills, conceived in short precise terms, like the modern Bills of Exchange; the faction of the Ghibellins being expelled Italy by the Guelphs, retired to Amsterdam, and used the same means for the recovery of their effects in Italy, as the Jews had done: from whence the Dutch Merchants took the hint of negotiating Bills of Exchange, and soon spread the practice throughout Europe."

Great Britain, the present Emporium of
Commerce, by the multiplicity of her Chan-
nels through which that Commerce flows, re-
ceives more of the Article in question than
any other Nation, or State, on the Globe, the
discounting of which, forms part of the Trade
of the Bank of England, and to no inconsi-
derable amount. It is computed by some Persons, who, by their transacting Business with
this Corporation, should be much better informed than myself on this head, that upon an
average, they discount to the amount of between Nine and Ten Millions Sterling per
Annum. A recent Publication states it at
Ten Millions,* and I should suppose the
Author would not have hazarded such an
assertion, without having a good foundation for
it. This Trade of Discount brings in no in-
considerable part of that profit, which supports
this immense Establishment; computed in all
the Departments to employ as Clerks, &c.
between 5 & 600 Persons.

* Letter to Mr. Alderman Curtis, then
Lord Mayor, by Mr. Simeon Pope, 1796.

Disquisitions have frequently occurred, whether the facility with which Discounts are in general obtained, have done most good, or harm, in the trading part of the Community : much has, and much may be said, in support of either side of the question ; but in order to come fairly at the merits of it, it ought to be observed, that there are two kinds of Discounts, the real, and the fictitious, or accomodatory : the first is, where the Gentleman Merchant, or Trader, having *real* Notes, or Bills of Exchange, in his possession, and finding it more to his advantage to have the present use of the Cash, than to wait until the Note, or Bill, becomes due, carries it to his Banker, or the Bank, for that purpose. The latter naturally divides itself into two parts, expressed by their respective titles, *fictitious*, and *accommodatory*, the first, upon supposed Credit only, without any real foundation, or property at the bottom, which quickly involves all concerned therein in one universal ruin, by the accumulation of interest ; but the other is materially different ; for although not quite-

what may be called real, yet if extended to
discreet and prudent Persons, it enables them
at sundry times to accomplish advantageous
Bargains, or Purchases of various denomina-
tions, and thereby to extend their Credit without danger, or hurt to any one : it is also certain that the easiness with which Discounts
have at times been obtained, has tempted
many People, even of the latter description,
to extend their dealings beyond what prudence
and discretion warranted, and thereby hurt
themselves and others ; but then this in general proceeded from not having duly considered the point they were aiming at, or the
Speculation in which they were going to employ the Money so obtained ; also from living
up to the full extent of their Capital, both real,
and fictitious, for so I call (in this instance)
that addition obtained by *accommodatory* Discounts; instead of confining their expences
within the bounds of the interest arising from
their *real* Capital only ; upon the whole, it
may be said, that Discounts under proper
regulations are of the utmost importance to the

Trading Interest; and that they are under proper Regulations by this Corporation cannot admit of a doubt, as they never discount but for those who are well known, or who keep Cash with them in their Banking Department, and by the care and precaution used therein, I have never heard that they were materially, if at all injured by failures. Their own Notes, upon which subject so much has been said, both in and out of Parliament, are founded upon such a solid Rock of real Property, as to render them co-existant with the Nation itself; *one cannot fall without the other*, so long as the just Demand of the Company upon the Government for 11,686,800l. remains unpaid; to which may be added the 10,847,568l. 13s. 7d. stated to be due to them, and unsatisfied on the 25th Day of December, 1796,* making in the whole the enormous Sum of 22,534,368l. 13s. 7d. but not to insist upon the latter, as by the coming in of the Land, and Malt Taxes, for the different Years, it

* See the Note, Page 34.

admits of fluctuation; still I am justified in my assertion of their fixed stability, by only taking their present substance, as stated by the many times before-mentioned Committee of the two Houses of Parliament in their first Report; which, if I state by way of Debtor and Creditor, will be more satisfactory, by appearing at one view.

The Bank of England, in Account current with the Government of England; and consequently with the Nation at large.

Dr.		Cr.
To Amount of *all Debts* and *Demands* upon this Corporation on the 25th day of February 1797, all the Bank Notes in circulation included. } 13,770,390		By Sundries, Cash, Bullion, Securities, &c. &c. } 17,597,280
To Balance, in favour of the Bank of England. } 15,513,690		By Debt due from Government, } 11,686,800
29,284,080		29,284,080

Thus it appears upon this fair and clear
ſtatement, that after paying EVERY DEMAND
UPON THEM; the Corporation are poſſeſſed
(if the Nation keeps faith with them) of a
clear Balance in their favour, of FIFTEEN
MILLIONS, FIVE HUNDRED AND
THIRTEEN THOUSAND, SIX HUN-
DRED AND NINETY POUNDS
STERLING; such being the fact, how can
any one, dare to queſtion their Solvency, or
endeavour to stigmatize them, by saying they
have stopped Payment; as well might a Debtor in any other common case, queſtion the
Solvency of his Creditor; which, if he did, I
fancy a Court of Law, would soon chastise
him for so doing: suppose for an instant, my-
ſelf was indebted to another Person Ten
Thousand Pounds; and in consequence of
my not being able to pay it, my Creditor was
obliged to stop Payment himself; ſhould I
not be the most ungrateful wretch in existence, if instead of doing all that was in my
Power, to alleviate his misfortune, and assist
G   him

him to the utmost, I should make it my Business to revile him in all places, scoff at those misfortunes, which I was the immediate cause of bringing on, and abuse him myself for having stopped Payment? and yet such is the conduct pursued by the Opposition in, and their adherents out of Parliament; and this Obloquy comes with by far the worse grace from those, who have been in former Administrations, and remain Members of the Legislature at this time; who must also know, that all they have said, and that all they do say upon the subject, is mere FROTH; without any real substance, or foundation. It may therefore be said, that whatever the Enemies of this country, either foreign or domestic, may endeavour to atchieve, yet such is the internal, and effective strength of this great Body, erected upon the solid foundation of REAL PROPERTY, that they may bid defiance to all *Maligners*, and must rise superior to all their *Machinations*.

I cannot

1 cannot make a better conclusion than by quotations from two Authors, to whoſe Works I am much indebted for many hints, and some matter, towards the construction of this small Work. Doctor Smith in his Wealth of Nations speaking of the Bank of England, ſays,

" The stability of the BANK OF ENGLAND, IS EQUAL TO THAT OF THE BRITISH GO-VERNMENT. All that it has advanced to the Public, must be lost, before its Creditors can sustain any loss."

And Mr. Rolt in his Dictionary of Trade and Commerce, under the Article Bank of England finishes by ſaying, *as if prophetic of the present Times :*

" Thus firmly established is this glorious superstructure of the national credit of Great Britain, having the Legislative Power of the Kingdom for its foundation ; a security sufficient

ficient for so noble, so extensive a fund ; a
security coeval with the liberties of the Peo-
ple, that cannot perish without the extinction
of Freedom, and which has SO CLOSELY
RIVETTED THE CONSTITUTION OF THE
BANK, WITH THE COMMON INTEREST OF
THE COUNTRY, THAT THEY SHOULD NOW
CO-OPERATE FOR THEIR MUTUAL PRESER-
VATION, AGAINST THE EXTENDED ARM OF
AMBITION, THE DESIGNING EYE OF AVA-
RICE, THE ENVY OF SURROUNDING ENEMIES,
AND THE FORCE OF FUTURE INVASIONS.

F I N I S.

This Day is Published, Price 1s. 6d.
By T. BOOSEY.

SECOND EDITION, WITH ADDITIONS,

A N

EPITOME OF THE STOCKS

A N D

PUBLICK FUNDS;

Containing every Thing necessary to be known
for perfectly understanding the Nature of
those Securities, and the Mode of doing
Business therein.

TO WHICH IS ANNEXED,

A COPIOUS EQUATION TABLE,

Exhibiting at ONE VIEW not only the ex-
act Value the different Stocks and Funds
bear, or ought to bear, with respect to
each other, but also with the Value of
Land ; and likewise the several Prices, at
which the same Interest is made in either
upon the Money laid out.

TOGETHER WITH AN

A P P E N D I X,

Containing the only Account ever yet published of the Bank Stock and Funds of the
United States of America.